WINTER'S LAST APPLE

POEMS
PROSE POEMS
MICRO-FICTION

KEN POYNER

ISBN: 979-8-218-22165-2

Grateful acknowledgement is made to the magazines in which many of these pieces originally appeared:

365 Tomorrows
Asimov's Science Fiction
Blue Unicorn
Cabinet of Heed
Café Irreal
Caffeine Presse
Club Plum
Conte
Damfino
Danse Macabre
decomP
Fear of Monkeys
Foliate Oak
Frigg
Full of Crow
Gnarled Oak
Grievous Angel
Headlight
Liminality
Linden Avenue
Marathon
Microfiction Monday
Misery Tourism
Mobius
Naugatuck Review
Open
Pacific Review
Palaver
Pank
Panoply

Red Fez
Riggwelter
Rune Bear
Sanitarium
Seine und Werden
Silver Blade
Star*Line
Steel Toe Review
Subliminal Interiors
Tiny Molecules
Unbroken Journal
Unlikely Stories

Contents

WINTER'S LAST APPLE

An empty morning rises with snow between our windows. The white pressing on our sills tries to slip under the stoic wood, and has its words for us. I hunger for the warmth of your thriving heart. I can see through the shatters of snow the outline of your small room – the table, the mirror, the closet door held ajar by your own flop-eared and grievously tempting closet monster, even the anthrax sealed envelope of your love's lasting love lying unopened – where surely you wait coiled in bed like a pity, dimly aware of the man across but a brief way: the man thinking in his metal idleness of your heart, and the warmth it might be in anyone's hands. No, in his.

A HISTORY OF BIOPHYSICS

Once a drawer of ghosts is filled
I shut it and connect the latch
So it will not slide unattended open.
Ghosts need their routine. So I fold
And catalogue. I note, about each,
Its circumstance of special attributes:
So many idiosyncrasies – but enough
Idiosyncrasies pooled, and the lot of them
Make a colossal ordinary. I cannot
Come to that conclusion too soon.
Each ghost for a while deserves
A modicum of respect. But it is
Inevitable – tray after tray of ghosts,
Each perhaps alone a haunting of merit;
Taken together in their great weightless mass
A background hum that is just the noise
Of the Universe coming, the Universe going.
It is my routine, and I know it.

ALLEGING ROMANCE

You assemble the car out of ordinary things: cabinetry, dining room chairs, a bed worn out, three chickens and an old dog from Henley's. Its engine is the heart of a bear. You draw the choke and the heart sputters, coughs itself into rhythm, pushes blood into the axles. You proudly slip into the barbed wire seat, pull a feather to signal you are entering the public street. On her porch, your future wife is turning over furniture, prying at loose boards – her long, rusting chain dress blindly seducing the broken porch light – her mouth worriedly wicking *where oh where is my thundering bear?*

CHILDREN IN THE RAFTERS

I hear they inhabit
The girders at the tops of unused warehouses,
Comfortable in the cramp
Of supporting joists and bracing beams, yet
Buffered by all the empty space below.
Even with rusted skylights and missing panels,
There is still enough dark left at the roof to eat them
Like the last of this week's groceries.
Listen: you can hear them shifting,
Swaying on the senile metal, wrapped
Four limbs around a weight bearing pylon:
A building and a subspecies indivisible.
I am not afraid of them. Some
Say they will drop molding ceiling tiles
On the unconcerned passing below,
Piss on your halo as you angel-step through.
My little brothers. At home in no home,
Watching the abandoned family abandoning,
Watching them scurry at ground level while,
Almost human, they claim the warehouse air
And the right to drop whatever they want.
I am always concerned, and when
I take the shortcut through this rotting post-worth
Construction, if I have one I drop
A penny or a nickel on the floor,
Sometimes the still grieving half
Of a cigarette. I imagine I can hear
The shadow excitement above me; and when
I come back through, as safe one way as
The other, always what I have left them
Is gone.

SEASIDE EMBRACE

I remember us at the beach. You wore one of those one piece bathing suits with the cut-out sides, and I had full shorts and a t-shirt. The rapt pier lights kept us far enough away. The water was muscling in crabs. The crabs started picking at the fish. Then, they noticed us. I could see their eyestalks waving. They collected themselves, claws clacking out what only just then I understood was language. You did not recognize it. I could not translate it for either of us, but I knew it was a terrible language of injury and dissolution and that surely its contents were directed at us. And then they came: dozens, perhaps hundreds, perhaps thousands. You did not see the danger, but, ever the dutiful lover, you ran when I said run and we sped parallel to the shoreline, a gathering of crabs carving the sand behind us. You seemed excited by your breathing. I was thinking we could not run with only the water at our side: we needed to turn and run inland. Likely you were never there and I have never been to the beach, but I have been smuggling crabs into the old barn out back, trying to translate the awful clack they make between themselves, a language perhaps speared at us: crabs clumsy but dangerous with their fearsome claws and untranslatable pounding speech. Understanding why we would be the subject of their conversations might be precious to us.

LETTER FROM THE
GREAT GRANDCHILDREN

Every day the sky is a bit farther off.
The waves by our place at the shore
Lack the crispness they once had.
There is always less to eat.

We still have husbands and wives,
Make children, mend fences,
Tend gardens, darn clothes,
Marvel at window glass.
I watched a man fishing in a swimming pool.
We are still unafraid to try new things.

We no longer keep pets.

Barter has replaced hard currency.
Each of us creates our own prices,
Shops around to establish the customary rate.
There is no lack of advice. Any neighbor
Will tell you when you have been taken advantage of.

Our hope sits by the fireplace
Hoping we will build a fire.
Wood is scarce, and burns quickly,
Its cellulose going slack in our developing circumstance.
No matter how much hope whines
We simply share each other's close company
Until the first of the heavy
Brown snow tatters in from the loosened North.

Schedule and prediction are dear to us.
We learned calendars can be recycled.
At first, we had the whole set right
And all the numbers matched. Now
It keeps the order of the months, nothing more.
We use the moon for accuracy,
The calendar for nomenclature,
And dream against its fanciful pictures.

Time to fish.
Time to salt.
Time to hunt.
Time to weave.
Time to forage.
Time to repair.

How simple our lives have gotten,
How less trivial. You would not recognize
Yourself in us.

Yesterday I met a stranger.
Was that so bold in your time?

THE SPIRITS OF KNOWLEDGE

The angels leave South Scotia. The religious turbulence there simply became too much for them. They leave their prized lions behind. By day, the lions sleep. With early evening, the lions hunt. It can be inconvenient for a citizen to be out and about early evenings. A collection is taken up to hire a chess master to train the lions in chess. Theory is: chess will give outlet to the lions' unleashed predatory instincts. What purposes the angels had for the lions is unknown, but it is hoped that chess, with its binary nature and twists of logic, will fill as well the need of purpose in the lions. The hired chess master leases the high school gymnasium and invites all the lions in for an early evening explanation of elemental chess. The master is less than two sentences into his introductory fundamentals lecture when the lions leap en masse and the man is totally consumed. The horror is universal. But South Scotia early evenings for the entire following week is safe. Certainly, a stray dog or cat is taken, but no neighbors go missing. A collection is taken up to hire another chess master. From the next town, settled in sacred ennui, the angels watch meticulously, looking for signs of learning, for intentions, for calm. They remember the time when they mastered lions.

FOREBODING

I slept once, casually, with a woman
who had three tiger tattoos on her back.
With the way she was dressed, I had not
seen them before. She offered no other
tattoos and except for her exceptional
willingness to be seduced was otherwise
unexceptional, a model of mediocrity.
The love making was most fierce
when she was atop, when
the tigers took to the air, wise
in the worth of her body. Afterwards
she slept naked on her side, the
tattoos scowling at me as though
I were not enough. I take my claim
back. I did not sleep.

TONES OF TREASON

I pass through the city of yellow houses. Hovels, ranches, duplexes, even apartment blocks. It wearies my eyes, a much harsher menu than the pleasant, leisurely background of my city of blue buildings. Yes, blue skyscrapers, blue warehouses, blue power plants, blue store fronts. Even the faces of good citizens seem to glow blue. All as easy on one's vision as tired children fresh from a sea-growth bath. I go unrecognized, unnoted, bent in the front seat of my without-obvious-purpose wagon. Who would suspect me? But if they knew what I surreptitiously carried through their city, they would fly at me like bears to riddled honey, or kites at war for limited air. My wicked wares sit under a tarp that does not clutter itself with attention, silent, perhaps nothing more than what numbs the salvage man's daily catch. And I am nondescript, invisible in application, a body holding up a collection of over-worn clothes, my steaming eyes downcast and sometimes only open one at a time. Soon I will be beyond the last yawning garish yellow house and safe on my way to the far brooding red village, where those apostate residents will greedily pick over my heresy of near vermillion shades and paints and dyes, offering me money, children, food, metal, pleasure in exchange: their no-mean brushes burnished, ladders already set against second-stories. Alabaster neophytes will scrape their skin and stand naked hoping for the dye that will bring them the red. I grandiloquently start my dark huckster's show, and hope no blue shows disapprovingly through.

SYPHILIS COMES TO THE SMALL ISLAND

We were unknown to each other but soon made acquaintance.
It is difficult not to be intimate, forty-seven
Men and one pot at the front of the ship, the
Head, and only two sides on a ship and the long,
Long hurling months of the whole of us starting out
Each with our expectations, our duties,
Each with our specialties, but in the end
All forced into each others' jobs, whatever
It takes to make progress, to go one more nautical
Mile. The sea so flat that the rough of it is welcomed and
So rough that the flat of it is welcomed and no one
Knowing the midpoint, the exact tottering of change, except
Possibly the Captain, who, as the best of us,
Still looked like a savage and we would pray every
Morning that we would not be savages nor would
He and that we brave and collected souls would not
Perish on the face of the deep, nor sink beneath it, nor
By Leviathan be devoured, nor that our provisions
Would run out and that we then might think of one another
As prey, though no man would forsake his Christian
Heritage and take into his mouth another man's
Flesh. We thought of the evils of our spirit and
How only the grace of God could save us from
Ourselves. And at times our own base natures
Were with us, and surely the demons of the air,
All those long months. All those salt
Filled days, those nights sleeping in another man's
Sweat. And then
Land. A great wash of clear beach, the sand
White as the throat of our Sovereign, the sand

Like fortunes of diamond ground for no good
Reason, the sand between our toes so unlike
The hardwood of the deck and the keep and the
Heat of it unsealing our blood that we had not
Known was sealed. The bounty of the trees and
Even the smallest of crabs and open fire and
The natives were no threat to us, having come
To see the claiming of their land for better purposes,
Our small boat itself the better of all their navies
And our ocean tested galleon something they had
Seen only in clouds and shadows and rituals to untrue,
Pagan gods that harrumphed and departed. So of their royal
Family we took the child of fourteen or so years seeming
Most agreeable from the land to the small boat to the awe of the
Ship as our gentle hostage, her finery but simple shells and
The crustacean arm of something we had not yet seen, no doubt
Native only to this land and soon to be the glory
Of our explorations at least until the next glory,
And we prayed for the bounty of small things and
When each man had had his fill of her over the side
She went limp and naked and serviced and worn out,
But we kept the shells and the crustacean arm and at first
Put them on the wheel but found, hey boys,
There are more where she and her handsome
Uncomplicated baubles came from and
Praise God it was a long voyage and ever
Lasting is His mercy: that he has provided us
Heathens to comfort us and sustain us and
Whose bounty is ours for the appropriation,
Having with us God and the Sovereign and soon
These natives will appreciate what it is
To be civilized by gentlemen in spite
Of how greatly worn we are from the crossing.

MILITARY HISTORY

This is the story wherein the tank says I am strong and I will protect you. I look at the protection and see it is made of metal and tracks and has a mouth folded into a tube that shouts with the voice of God. I draw my hand along its musculature and it hums of self-possession. Anyone watching would see a man and a tank leaning against one another, and each already knowing each. Strength runs in many species, becomes its own greedy genius. With protection, I can make my strength a howl in the mighty night that frightens perhaps even the tank. So I accept the offer, discover the mumbling hatch, and join the tank. Outside, those who were watching a man and a tank lean together, now see only the tank. And there is only the tank. It is alone and strong and channels the voice of God. The man is already forgotten. I am forgotten. This is the ending of the story, wherein the tank persists. There is only the tank and the tank's quiver of intentions. What of the man? Maybe I am not he.

PHYSICS

Dark matter, my love.

I spin in your circles,
I loathe your gravity:
Yet I come back to you,
As a woman seeking
Forever the grace of her abuser,
Lying to herself,
Hating the lies, comforted
By their familiarity.

Dark matter, my love.

I sense your theory ever around me,
The embrace of the possible,
Or only the likely, your coldness
All in this world I need,
The beginning of me, and the end of me.
You seep into my existence
And I am replaced with your
Unforgiving.

Dark matter, my love.

I am unknown in your universe.
Control me. Compel me.
Know that I am
What you become, how
You sense yourself: the softly glowing hair
That colorlessly bristles as time brushes
Your long, universe hoarding arms.

See the light of me.
I am your only thought.

THE DEATH OF FRANZ FERDINAND

The fire that would be the world at last scorches you. It is then you notice the smoke and smell, the children running about with ash on their collars, the men in asbestos jackets, the women with licks of flame in their dresses as they go laughing by, the dogs running in polluted circles with fire tied to their tails. The oxygen is being sucked out of your living space and you think can no one put out this fire? Where is the fire department, where are the stilted firemen, where is the loving hydrant? Ah, but this is the fire becoming the world. No municipal budgets exist that can fund an alternative to it. You have to agree to burn, to watch all that you have be consumed as the world. You demand to know who started this fire becoming world, what citizen assassin? Why were you not told? Perhaps it was a collective decision, metered out like the bonded yards of a pyrotechnic symphony. Blame yourself. And what do you think you would have done, instead? Be careful not to fool yourself: you would have urinated in circles on the embers just so the world could never be, unless it would be made of steam.

THE DISAPPEARANCE OF THE BEER TRUCK DRIVER

They faked my death.
Stole someone else's body,
Fudged all the records, falsified
X-rays and dental prints. I went
To South America and opened a bar.
There was a funeral and real people spat
Real tears, my family was worked up,
Collected the life insurance, no
Questions asked. I was still
On the payroll. Years later
My daughter would blame her early pregnancy
And shallow marriage on the lack of my presence,
Come to believe I had died
Just to keep her life from being successful.
I cashed the checks, kept the accounts,
Hired a crown breasted local to tend bar.
I talked to the expatriates and looked
Like someone they once knew. I bet
More than a few of them had died, too.
My wife
Four years later remarried. It was
No one I had known. The company
Always knew where I was, needed
The address to send my unchanging salary.
I think a few of my alleged customers
Were merely sent to see how I was doing,
If I were happy enough, if the trade
In lives had gone well enough that at least

I wouldn't make waves. I guess
It has, but being dead sometimes really sucks.

THE MAN WHO PAINTED HIS WIFE RED

What should he do with the red paint? Before he took it from the paint store he had thought he wanted the color blue. But then he realized he had no plan for what was going to be done with the paint; so, as he thought about the paint itself in ever more detail, what color paint he would take became less an option than a serendipitous outcome, and he began to focus on the body of the actual theft, the many distinct steps in the process. A quart, a gallon, a five-gallon barrel? One container, yes, but what size container? Perhaps he would choose by the ethereal esthetics of the label. And once a prize is selected: out the backdoor, or straight through the front door? Mix the purloined paint in with other legitimate purchases, a hidden conquest in with the properly enrolled? Dodge innocently away with the paint concealed within his jacket? Drop a shoulder and run full-out, knocking over an out-of-frame incoming patron? And the security cameras. This most perfect of thefts must be filmed. Every moment of it. Employees for years will have to watch the video, be lectured on how to recognize even grandly accomplished petty criminals. They will endure being told: see how he cases the aisles, see how he comforts the merchandise, see how he calms security with his eyes, see how he consumes the air of each yawning exit. Overly confident managers will say: let this splendid artist keep the paint; the lessons of this video will serve us much more.

THE DISCOVERERS

Everything was going well.
We had met the natives
And they were hospitable.
We feasted on unfamiliar fruit,
The juice of it running down
Our humbled chins to the delight
Of our unevolved hosts. We showed them
How a cigarette lighter works,
Broke into well staged dark with a flashlight.
The chief began to describe
How fine his ripening daughters were
And we were untimid in our thinking
Of what might likely come next.
We were a civility of broad gestures.
But then, just above the head
Of one of the royal family's lesser wives,
We saw a conversation bubble.
Luridly white, considering the background,
And tussled with pitiably black letters,
It hung above her like a hole in the
Chicken wire of our bedrock industry.
She was not even speaking to us,
But rather to a boy lurking annoyingly
At the tripping edge of our celebration.
None of us could make out what was written.
But soon there was another one;
And then yet another. Simple fork
And tray conversations, open the door
And let in some air conversations.

Each speaker was going from aural to word
Bubble. And then we espied outside
That the shadows were just cross hatch
On flat medium, some not even connecting
Properly to their subjects, and the sunlight
Blocked was as dull as day old dishwater.
Our host by then was speaking all in cartoon bubbles,
And his edges were growing more
Into dark lines, the fill being a wider brush,
Certain parts of him fading into incomplete.
And we thought: oh no, not the daughters.
But we could not look, and in our laps
Watched instead our own ink shimmy and stink
And refuse to soak into our pants.
I have been trying to say I cannot fathom
What has happened to us; but you
Just cannot draw fast enough, you cannot
Pull out the right pernicious pencil, cannot
Manage, with backing capital, the fill; but, please,
Try harder.

THE RAIN MISTRESS

She flicks an ash from her cigarette over her left shoulder. It passes the breathing tattoo of a thunder cloud on her arm. It jostles her barely concealed right breast, the one that the teenage boy at the bar has been unprofitably staring at since she mightily sat down. "Everything is about moisture," she says. Outside, you can hear the dust rubbing away the will of the wooden structure, challenging brick and stone to a likely hobo dance contest. Why, after prayer and sacrifice, do real rain makers have to be configured like this one? Word is, she was sleeping with Tom last night, and with Tom's widow the night before. She gets up, kicking over the chair – not in defiance but in brazen accident - taking a last draw of her beer, tossing the cigarette still alight on the bar, sashaying with a hip tide that pulls all the blood from every man's fingertips and sends it elsewhere. She fills in her gamboling outline with concrete. Economically she pushes dangerously through the arid, near-shimmering door. When it is open, we can see already the skies are gathering a questioning dark, the wind is protectively cradling its testicles. She steps onto the porch and begins a debauched, rising moan. We are quietly pleading: bring rain or not; just say what you have to say, do what you have to do, then let us down gently. A bead of sweat forms on her feathering forehead and no one believes the sentences of the near thunder, only that the thunder is hiding something.

THE QUEUE

You've got to be the last one
To get something. The first
Is always pushy, larger,
Able not only to get to the head
Of the line, but able to keep
The position. It doesn't matter
What they are handing out:
Vaccines at a free clinic;
Bread from the back of a truck;
Peanut butter almost expired
From the last loading door
Of a long line of loading doors
Behind a supermarket warehouse.
Anything you can line up for,
Anything for which a line
Is the proper and orderly reaction.
Behind that first, most aggressive
Person in line is a small constellation
Of persons almost as pushy, almost as aggressive
As the first, but perhaps not willing
To waste energy – knowing that for
This much length of the line there will be
Enough. After all those
Who have taken a forward place, are those
Who occupy a place. Factually, all of us
Are in the line, too. And the object
Is to be the one with something in hand
When the giver says *no more*.
The pushers and the rowdies will be gone

And behind you will be all those
Who have waited in feral anxiety,
Though not fully sure they wanted anything:
But a few will look at you – you
Standing with your blanket or bread
Or sleeve rolled up – and those few
Will imagine how lucky you are,
How *enough* is linear, how *want* is a point.

THE STONING OF THE CLOWN

An army of clowns, yes. But this one clown, stabbing reds and glow-worm orange, whiteface and oversized lips: he stands out more pointedly for being alone. He could be on his way to a child's birthday party or a bank robbery or a members-only fetish-themed orgy. The fact that he is the only one makes him sternly suspect. With a clutch of mates, each perhaps festooned in different columns of clownware, small talk pressed between them like pebbles, no one clown would seem imperfect, beyond the dimension, or of ungainly motivation. But this lone conundrum: no matter his mission, he is up to no good. He presents himself, in his bearing, as prepared. No one is good enough to imagine pulling off an act of precise clownery alone, unless he does so not in public. Yet here he is, ambling unselfconsciously by the construction site where the macadam and sidewalk have been pulverized and wait for removal. All the concrete and rock-asphalt piled and preventing momentarily the onset of the new. He goes unthinking by and some fellow walkers wonder why he is so determined, why his costume does not humble him, what he has in his painted mind yet imagined to be done. And nearby, so much available rubble.

THE ORB

Yes, the sudden tour stop.
Those fresh antiquities, the ones
Just like the ones
In the mysterious guidebook. An offer
Of help. Our four-by-four
In the bleeding sun too long,
The radiator sputtering and
Our entire fresh water supply
Traded bottle by spurned bottle for
Distance. No thought, then,
Of thirst, of the walk to civilization,
Or something near and nearly like it. But no,
An offer of help.
Whose flag is that anyway?
Those antiquities are not antiquities
At all, and I told everyone —
You remember, everyone —
That no good would come of our good.
I tell you, we are in some fix,
Some construction of events that all of us
Are beginning to see as quite extraordinary,
Quite unlikely, quite statistically
Aberrant. Alright.
The main narrative bellows to someone
Else. Here is where I notice
Our companion in short-shorts —
Her unspeakably clean dark hair
Fallen over one eye and
Arched Biblically – has shaved

Her legs recently.
I am not that kind of man,
But it fits, don't you see:
It all comes together.
This is where I am meant to be
Though I never meant to be here.
This sudden tour stop.
The couple on holiday. The paperweight
Antiquities. Our justified thirst.
The foreign flag. The substantial
Woman, who turns out to be the sex-draped
Coincidental skeleton that blunts my selfish suspicions.
I am waiting for you to acridly
Unearth what is on the next page,
To flip ahead and see how many
Chapters are left to our beloved hero,
Whichever one of us our hero reveals himself to be.
One of you, insert action here.

THE PRIZE IN THE FOLD

Proof of the interdimensional love affair is scant. A sheet torn into scarves. A lone wine glass twisted into a blossom. Whispered condemnations coming from a closet. Perhaps the greatest proof is the emotional attachment placed on voids. Inference. She can turn one way and disappear. He can turn another and be suddenly too weighty to bear. What a trouble it must be for them. People imagine their sexual encounters to be like birds at a bird feeder in the rain. One man is doing a thesis on the mathematics of the likely affair. He will supply a proof of the possibility, though no one can prove the actuality. If there is an affair, it must be one steamy stream of numbers, algebraic symbols, balances. But most of us are sure of the ether-crossing, hauntingly physical affair. See the two of them together, one lightning in a bottle, one just lightning. Moments in our dimension, moments in another. You can almost measure them hand in hand, energies cascading toward affection and lust. Your vision is a flat picture at first. And then one of them turns.

THE END OF ACHIEVEMENT

Just beyond the flower garden at the end of the world.
Like the kind words you say
About someone you cannot remember.
As if in the moment of sexual climax
Together with someone you do not like,
Would not meet for dinner or take
To breakfast: not the perfect body,
Not the secret knowledge of you.
As though living in this generation
That will guarantee through its excesses
The destitution of its grandchildren.
Unsure if the well-groomed prey is prey
Or is actually the hunter doing very well,
Very well. That moment.
Change returned at a cluttered tourist shop
In a currency you do not understand,
The clerk smiling and a stain
From anywhere on his left breast pocket.
Your hand knowing what to do
Without you, without stoically consulting you:
Flawlessly, doing what it wants
And it is what you want, even
What you need. In this moment
Everything matters, everything
Is pounding at the glass of your
Kitchen window, bathroom window,
The sweet back glass of your sedan,
A full world with its own
Plans as you are watching,

The impulse, the parasympathetic tic,
Your hands independently in your lap,
Simply watching. And it is gone.

CONSTITUTION

For weeks we repaired our nets from the last thrashing. In man-mauling canoes and bell-bottomed barges last season we fought prevailing winds and a surf that despises us to take, in these nets, our many sins out beyond the reef to unfractured blue waters and toss them in. The process is simple but not clean. A sunning shark of greed here, slothfish baring its gills lethargically in the shade. Overbearing groupers stuffed with gluttony, unable to move, gasping for more, easy to capture but hard to lift. Ashore, we stuff nets full of sins, tie a woven ball of inequity. We line the shoreline with those nets; then mete out boats, load the sins, escape in a trial or two the prudish shallows and head for deep, unroiled water. At the right spot, we untie each net and spill each sin nakedly into the sea. Some sins will have torn through the mesh and flap loose in the boats. Each captain has a child on board who can reach into the small, cluttered spaces where an able vice can hide. Afterward, nets must be repaired. The sins have broken the weave and beckoned holes. Weeks we weave, an industry double quick. We must cast the nets whole when we return to the water, trawling, trawling, pulling from the deep our shriven sins again. So many sins, schools of pink shimmers with fins folded reverently. Shivering, ecstatic, waiting to be predatory again. Which will become avarice with cavernous jaws open again, which will entangle us with barbels of lust? The sins will strain the nets in return no less than the voyage out, and our repairs must make the nets strong again. Weaving haunts us like sex, weaving is breath, weaving is our gauntlet of everything.

ACCOMPLISHMENT

Given the job of opening the rocks,
He stares at each one, turning them,
Searching for edges. He rubs
The dust from several and sights
Along the crystal grain. He bangs
Two together, then stands
On a pile to drop one at better height
To the sounding floor. He scratches a few
With dissimilar faces together.
Eventually, he tries biting.
The foreman can see this is not working.
After lunch the worker is told
His progress is less than optimal,
But no matter: everyone has
An aptitude, a talent to apply,
And the trick is to match
The necessary occasion to the mentor
Who can illuminate the path to uncoiling it.
He is led into a room reeking of near
Capacity humidity. His glasses fog
And his clothes drop damp against his skin.
Across the way he sees four vast vats,
Each more than ten men could lift,
The air above them a cold mist.
The foreman points out the vat nearest
And tells him he should burn the excess water.

Tomorrow is nothing more than the next day, but tonight
His dreams will be alight with burning rocks
Adrift on vast, unlocked, gloriously open oceans.
This is his calling.
This is the noble thing he can teach others.

BRIAN, AT THE WATER

The voice spread out like ocean drain in a shoe box, "Brian!" It was coming from all sides, emerging from the tributaries with its shields of clamshell, scuttling from the beaches like horseshoe crabs wondrously intact. Yelling for a child, something commonplace, something the dead would do if they had not died. Who is this Brian? What is he being called to do? Have his dinner? Come to go to the store? Apologize for the thump he applied to his sister? Or perhaps he is older, not the child, but the husband. The voice sloshes about, wiping the jetty clean, eating stray pollen. Perhaps the lawnmower awaits. The clothesline has come unstuck from the backyard again. The office, so sorry, briefly needs him. Or the in-laws have left, the house is dark and moist, as alone as oysters in a reef: this will be the name of the one we should now in a carnal rage make. And so the voice rocks and rages and reaches like a blue crab claw searching for the rim of the pot as the water begins to boil. I want to be Brian, the conception or the completion. I want to drown that humiliating voice.

CIVIC DUTY

We hear the shooting of citizens
In the street one block over
From our apartment complex.
Twelve units. Thirteen, if you count
The never rented one room sitting off
By itself, barely under our roof.

It is a formal shooting.
Multiple guns, all fired as one.

We cannot see from here
If they use a wall or use
The street itself or the sidewalk,
Nor what, if anything, they do
With the bodies afterward.

We are too far away

To hear whether they read charges
Or make accusations. We do not
Know if they are using multiple teams
Or simply have an abbreviated
Firing squad procedure. We assume
From the pace and slow movement
Of the noise that they are taking
Everyone in turn. We
Set out extra food for our cats,
And there are no dogs allowed
In our building. We wait our time.

JOB PERFORMANCE

It is time to bring more virgins to the ogre. I don't think he knows whether they are virgins or not, but he has read, in the virgin-eating-ogre manual, that he eats virgins and so he assumes that such is what we bring him. He always works strictly by the book. This is his first job as a small-town local virgin-eating ogre – he wants to get the job done just right, perhaps earn a letter of recommendation when he moves on. Little chance. Two cycles past we slipped in a mother of two and last cycle we pushed a many-times over grandfather. This will be his last cycle here. The town has already voted to sack him. He gets his termination letter as soon as he finishes off this batch. I want to be there to see him delightfully fill his emptiness and then learn, ineptly sated, he has to move on.

LAST CHANCE DINER

It never intended to be the last.
The original idea was that
Block by block the town
Would build out, suck up the scrub,
Spewing development, be eventually
So much commerce and tax revenue
That it would at first be called
A city, and then be administratively designated
De facto such. But at this exact point
The scheme ran dry. Dry. Dry,
For no reason anyone knows.
No particular shame owed to this
Last property. A fine property, once.
Yet, no establishment can long stand
In good faith against the fact
Of being the end of a town, the gateway
To the wilderness. Inevitably,
The paint fails to renew. The window
Leaning closest to oblivion
Sticks open. The HVAC works
Half the year, you pick which half.
The old red truck on the left
Side of the once even parking lot
Has been there for six years, unsalvageable,
And now trademark of the place.
Go in, and you will find
The menu inaccurate, two
Booths marked off as closed for repair,
The raised glass topped cake display

Empty. When the waitress comes around
A counter three nails short of complete
She will not greet or offer, she will say,
"What brings you here?"

HIS PLAN

In walks the gnome. We had been looking for him for two weeks. No success. No sight of his towered green hat. No sound of his horn-toed shoes. No whiff of his unwashed character. We had burst into citizens' suspicious homes, turned over people's closets, looked in attic-deposited boxes way too small to hold a gnome, trafficked under beds. We had combed the trunks of junked cars. We concluded no one in town was intentionally hiding him. In an attempt to draw him out, we penned his unicorn in the closely mown town square, published an auction date. No show. We listened for the tap of his gnarled cane on sidewalks, planks and ceilings, telling all good townsfolk who might normally use a cane for the nonce not to do so. No luck. We watched from hidden blinds the house where his reputed girlfriend lives – a full bodied blonde who could hide nothing, not even ideas: her house luxuriating the dust of its own degeneration, with any fresh boards not matching the past loosely dangling history of the sanctuary, the roof a dear friend of rain, the best of its days bundled and latched as scrap for anyone's fire. And now, here he, eerily substantial, is: fresh shaven, nearly bathed, the cane left behind. Then, most moving of all, he starts - his fairy money still good this side of the rift in dimensions - paying off everyone's bar tab. The bartender sullenly makes his change in four-dimensional sterling. Molly, the stereotype at the end of the bar, slides a little more his way. We will never be rid of him. For all, another round to drown our responsibility.

FRUITION

The city was waiting in less than its best dress.
Streetlights were embarrassed but dutiful.
Early morning deliveries tried to synchronize their sounds,
And failed. A man looking for a lost cat
Realized he searched unfamiliar streets,
Unknown neighborhoods. The city
Bided its time, regarded the length
Of its nails, bit its tongue.
Our power plant became ever hungrier.
Day old bread became two days old.
Who needs suburbs anyway? The city
Waited. Finally, a girl in a green dress
Began walking at one end of Main Street.
No, she skipped. She danced.
The lost searching man did not see her,
But evening pickup trucks synchronized their noises,
The power plant ate a slug of coal.
She pranced, she wriggled, she sashayed.
In her arms, a cat.
And all the front porches
On all the houses of the city
Said in green envy, a cat once lived here –
But not this specific cat. Until the next
Day, the wait was over. You can stop dancing.

FIT

I am no good at ice fishing. I drill the holes too small: only large enough to get the hook and bait through to the water. When a fish takes hold, I tie the line off and come faithfully to get you. I love to watch you weather yourself into boots and coat and knit cap and run like a deep water crab through the snow to where the fish, under ice, struggles against my knots, your attending axe having been used in your locomotion like a cane. And then you sumptuously attack the ice, spending more energy than the eating of the fish will ever return. Sometimes, the vigor of your work shakes the fish free; yet, often the hole grows open like a blizzard's mouth and out comes the fish and none of them look as good or as cunning as me, the first you hacked unthinkingly into the air.

FLOW, THE CITY SUMMER

I'm down by the fire hydrant that never opens

Waiting for your body. You may come
Or not. What I want is that sidling
Walk, that hip-filled locomotion, the tip
Of the shoulders that brings one breast
Up and then down and then the other up
And then coldly down. I want the stripes of your
Cheap dress to run sideways across
Your body and the strict straight
Of your hair to compete with the cloth,
To fall shoulder length and make its
Statement against the prideful dress like two
Girls fighting in an alley over a boy
Too full of himself to fill either one of them.
My hands would be the shy fists of all three.
I'm down here, by the fire hydrant.
Maybe if your body joins me, I can finally
Pry the cover off this summer boil,
Sweat tuned hydrant, and let the water
Spit sinfully over us, matting your scored dress:
With your elegantly simple nipples underneath
Pimped by the damp cloth and the purely
Delicious fur at the grip of your Y
Shouting you can come or not; the water
Rolling off of my bare chest and the fur
Of my stomach slicked in a line and
Me not waiting at all, not even here:
Just my body, and the low sounds

Of a hydrant pushing angrily against its cap,
Thinking that if it had help it could
Explode and like shrapnel be nothing but action.
I am like that. I can show you explosions.

Bring your body down.

DISTANCE

Being a hammersmith in a village of glass people is not as unprofitable as you might think. For the most part, citizens avoid heavy objects, take special caution with force and heft. I craft my hammers with care, making sure the balances are precise, the surfaces smooth. A glass customer does not want such a tool too easily leaning into inaccuracies. You might think there would be no market at all, that my creations would be anathema, a danger too far. But my wares sell almost as fast as I fashion them. People come alone to the shop's backdoor, wait until no one can see them in their light starved curled approach. Eyes to the left, eyes to the right, a complete reconnoitering spin. If they cannot see me, they call to see if I am in, a question that rises in tone towards its end, thinly hopeful. When I come, they silently lift a number of the available hammers, balance them, take practice swings. In a telling haste, they settle on one, place it in a grocery store sack they have brought as disguise, pay in cash and often do not wait for change. They try to keep their facial expressions out of the light. But I know the range of emotions leaking from them. Jealousy, envy, rage, drumming desires of larceny. What wonderful sins my handiwork can be put to in a kingdom filled with glass subjects! I supply the tool, adjust my working molds, and deaden my ears to glass breaking. I concentrate on my skills.

RIOT AT THE NIGHTCLUB

Everyone was just about as drunk
As staying vertical would allow
And that's when the Vampire hookers
Walked in: diaphanous gowns
Nearly see-through and six inch
Heels, and everyman was thinking
Do I have enough left in me
To hold out until sunrise? A pint,
No more, and with a day's rest
Another satisfied customer back
Pale, but looking for more. God
Forgive me, thinking of their cold
Persisting no matter the rush,
I grow stiff as a fish hook
And loosen my collar. We flex
Carotids and dance with them
At arm's length, make centuries old
Small talk. They reserve their strength,
Dip and suggest, as only millennia of
Bloodless coquetry could teach them. Winning
The top is every man's dream. They hint
A subservience everyone knows is not
There, a practiced fictional deference,
A guilty feral innocence. And then,
Like every night, someone trips, drops
A glass or drags his arm too close by
One of the vampire's ruby laced nails and there is
Technicolor on the comforting black and white,
There is blood.

THE RATIONALE

Between us there is notice. A braille of recognition, a mummery of portraiture. You expect cycles of me, rumors of left-handed gods, a great passion for ingestible stones. Mine is the part of meeting expectations. Yet expectations supplely oppress you. And here I am wingless, and for the full moon grieving sinful, rich feathers. Feel them. Take one and split it into a quill. Dip it into the dark and write for me your love for another. Excuse all, reveal nothing – but write the confession with me, quill by quill. Write not of me, but through me only. Here, take another. Soon, rumors of deified stones.

THE REFUSAL OF THE RAIN

You would think it would come
On letterhead, impact printed,
On folded high rag content bond,
A red seal of wax impressed
With the image of a brooding storage cloud.

A quick, smiling, always ready
To bow or nod or please, messenger
Holding the epistle next to his chest
With all of his fingers and the thumb
Opposed, should hurry with it
On foot through market streets
And under drying shopkeepers' laundry:
Bounding up official steps
With all the motion contained in his hips,
His shoulders set. The envelope

Should be oversized and the flap
Merely tucked in, the name of the
Intended recipient written grandly in ink
With unnecessary, but respectful,
Flourish, and stray calligraphy epiphanies.

When it is delivered, the selected bureaucrat
Should thank the bent and attentive
Messenger, carefully draw out the envelope's flap
And shake the message free, at the last using
A privately maintained pen knife to scrape
Clear the clarion red seal, confidently
Unfolding the rare paper to read
With only one creased eye:

Drought.

THE GIANTS OPEN DOORS

All the doors of the road are open. Someone must have left them unlocked. Or maybe there is a skeleton key. Or someone was willing to pry them open through unleavened force. No matter. You cannot drive on this road: all its doors are open. For now, I will let the baffled, thirsty commuters ponder the problem. Twisted in their conundrum they will fret and opine and venture into today's nervous rain to test the latches, look about the litter surrounding the doors and their frames for clues. But not I. I say solve a problem with a problem. Bring two irritations to one smoothing. I say: turn it over to the giants. They have power and perspective and too long have been grumbling about being out of work, idled as though fairy tales were no longer good currency. Let them apply their frustration to the open doors. It will be work enough to keep them from doing stray harm, from setting off to inflame the rocks or pull out the ocean's nails. And it will make them believe we still need them.

THE LOVERS

You are the alligator in my bathtub:
What you might eat of me
Is different in this environment
Than if we met in the reed shallows
Of some great lake where children
Go to gig frogs.

Those children plan to gig enough frogs
That dinner for the whole family -
A family weary from the bottomless day of tending
And herding and washing and gossip
And bearing and ceremonial conflict -
Is gathered with simply one lone sharpened stick:

And then together they disappear.

THE PURSUIT OF HAPPINESS

A man marries a train, and decides he will be most fond of the observation car. The glass sides, the lithe, thin ribs of support. He keeps a rumble in his heart for the other cars, and all the ordered elements of his train. But none are as light and unnecessary as the observation car. None holds the certain death of imagination, replacing it formally with the face of what is unconcernedly going past. Why is it connected other than for the guttering pleasure of travelers? The man thinks, we would be less a loving couple without this gleaming observation car. So it does have its purpose, after all. The man thinks: in the gauge of our locomotive passion each night when I count the cars cautiously, I count that car twice.

THE TRAIL

As you unfold the paper you realize
It is an appointment note,
One that will drag you all by itself
To the next wait station where
Your expectations will be met by a man
With two ice cream cones, one half eaten,
The other pushed forward for you.
Meet me. Please.
This is all that I know how to do.
Next stop it will be coffee,
And there will be a cute dog in a sweater
At the end of a red leash that for no real
Reason is red, but meet me. Please.
Unfold each piece of paper like
You do not know what it is going to say.
Read the directions once again and tip slightly
Forward, refold the paper, look
Over your left shoulder.
Meet me. Please.
We will be good for one another.
Anonymously our dry air
Will share time like old, tired raincoats.
Our hearts will beat sympathetically.
Meet me. Please.
I am the red paint bucket
Of your imminent arrival.
This is the sum.

THE TRUCE

The air is fresh from the last rain. This air feels as humble as any air finding itself in a clearing in a long stumbling wood. The mosquitoes angling above the encircling trees fly unconcerned in to the armistice table with a grandiose, unnecessary arc. When they at last sit, for each mosquito one set of legs splays across the table, one set putters in their laps, one set dangles down from the ill-fitting seats. Across the table, a man, his two wives, a servant nervously squirm in their mass-manufacture chairs. Smaller mosquitoes above swirl in the air like child-tossed confetti. On the table there is a sheaf of papers in front of each participant, held against the breeze by a blot of amber. Wind plays at the edge of the pages, makes no progress. The man, moving as slowly as the fall of dry leaves, pulls a ballpoint pen from his starched shirt pocket and signs the top page of the sheaf of papers before him, reservedly pulls the paper from the stack and slides it to the bottom, resettling the amber. One mosquito bends forward and using his over-sized turgid proboscis signs a corresponding paper in residual blood. All the papers will be signed, but at the conclusion of this first pair of signings, one wife rises, goes to sit at the side of the nearest mosquito. The servant moves that wife's untouched set of papers to her new seat. The partisans spattered in the woods move closer.

THE WEALTH OF NATIONS

I can win this competition.
Other men
Will begin to question
The value of the prize,
The glamour in being the man
To sit longest on the ice,
Guarded by only a thin set of britches,
And nothing more.
Their bottoms will grow ingloriously cold.
The blood will pull from their backsides,
Seep away from their lower limbs. Their extremities
Will shut down as the body's heat
Is shifted plaintively to the chest and head.
Each man, alone, will question
The utility of this competition,
And his practical place in it.
Over all
The digital timer will seem too slow,
Looking as though it would radiate warmth —
But instead drawing it out of everyone, a black
Hole of intention, taking from each man
The special character that would make him
Sit here on the ice, strive to be the last sitting
This year,
Just as someone was the last someone sitting last year.
This year, I can win this competition.
I can focus my eagerness, focus my understanding
That each man here thinks he can outdo me:
That it is he and not I who has

The stamina or courage or
Ability of steel self-sacrifice that will
Make for the win.
How much time does it take: and whose time?
I will the clock forward,
And every man wills the clock forward,
Looking for the first competitor to break:
Our hearts slowing to the cold,
Our minds jettisoning our unapplied memories;
All of us bound together as one
Numbing brotherhood, and each of us yet
With that singularly warm, insulating idea of winning.
Surely it is my idea that smolders the brightest.

POOL

Your job is to tend the herd of giraffes that lounge in the median of Granby Street. You bring water and food several times a day, and that is the time most likely when a traffic tie up will occur. Motorists stop to see them knuckle down for water or stretch for the suspended food. Sometimes a motorist will not stop, but, fascinated, will drift into the median, begin to mix with the giraffes. Already this year one animal has been put down by car strike. Nonetheless, it counts as an accident. You hardly ever win the monthly accident prediction pool. By far, the red-river hogs four streets over cause the most accidents: pushing drivers to swerve out of the hogs' random ways, or in their bull-headed fury charging a car, which then goes careening off like a plug in a pinball machine. With giraffes, most accidents are passive, whereas the hogs add in a goodly slop of aggression. But an accident is an accident, and they all count. Every month I have a chance of winning.

SOUNDING

That is what I remember: the canoe,
Unsteady in the water, the paddle
Suspended, and my horrible listening
Against a water waiting flat as a mother-in-law's
Mirror. You cannot come here with me.
You say that you can, but in saying this
Your mouth grinds the air like
A boat's roughly hacked prow
Rushing the sand of an island's beach;
And I am already believing
That yes, that was the sound. That
Single sound and
No other like it. I had been
Listening; and then rising to me
Was that one sacred sound
That I passionately, unwisely, imagined
To be despotically unnatural. And
I dipped the tip of the oar ever so
Emotionlessly into the water,
The lone actor with his lone action,
And it was gone.
You were with me.

EXPECTATION

Julio got a new tube of darkness. A week ago he squeezed the last one dry, rolling it in as tight a curl as manageable to force out the last of the black persuasion. With the new tube he heads out to where he earlier had been working, finding his previous dark swathe and the merely dim border he could make when his last tube began to sputter. Now he can squeeze a bit onto two fingers, thicken the unswerving border, apply the dark to the landscape and fixtures, the plants and people and pets. Even the insects and microbes of the air as they go by, come unsuspectingly within reach, are darkened. He works slowly, savoring the process, consummate in his art. His sphere of dark cautiously expands. At times, Julio inspects his work, retouches areas where the dark is too thin, where the swirls he makes in applying the dark come out as recognizable ridges. His dark must be even. People admire the growing dark and they prefer to stay in the dark if Julio has painted them there. If they emerge from the dark they move non-descript and shadowy about their business, no regaining of the shriven light. Julio assures them they will always be welcomed in the dark, they need no further coating. He begins to roll up the loose of his new tube of darkness, like a tin of expiring toothpaste. He frowns. No tube ever lasts as long as he wishes.

CITY OF RESOLVE

I went down to the corner store
and bought a crate of monsters.
The largest crate I could carry,
and twice I had to set it down
on the narrow sidewalk to rest
before I made it all the way
home.

I let them loose in my room.

Don't worry. Many people around here
do this. It is sort of a town
welcome ritual. The monsters leap out
and wrestle each other, bash
the furniture, try
to get into the closet – but mostly
settle with attacking the poor citizen
who bought and liberated them.

Most do not survive.

Citizens, I mean. The monsters
finger all the citizen's belongings,
mill about the citizen's room,
look in the kitchen, eat
in the backyard the startled dog.

By morning they report back to the store.

CONSISTENCY

There is not a lot of compromise available with an ice wife. The relationship revolves, strangely, around you. There is only one pliable point of view, one decision, one schedule. There is no warmth in the pairing. Passion is an admission of how long one can abide the cold. But you are your own master. Composed in ice, for her there is not a range of emotion, not a continuum of elaborations – just each day's facts, the physics of water and blind temperature. The simplicity, on the other hand, is alluring. There is nothing in an ice wife to force a change in your initial patterns, or her coy receptions. Once you have adapted, you have adapted. The way it is, is the way it will be. Settle in. Wait for spring.

DEVELOPMENT

When we found the tiny people
They were making civilization
In an uncivilized gully no one
Had thought to explore the value of

Except for them, and now us.
You can wonder why they would inhabit
Such an out of the way place, but
If this land of theirs were so easily
Reached, it would have long before now

Become ours, not theirs. There looks to be
Four, maybe five dozen of them,
Two long houses only three feet across,
A smattering of outbuildings. I can't imagine
At eight inches high they would farm.
Speculation is that they hunt the indigenous bugs

As we might hunt bison or deer,
Have a use for the exoskeletons, fashion
Beetle legs to brace roofs perhaps. Could be
There is insect worship, a place
Where souls are reborn as larvae; or no.
At this point in our knowledge, possibility
Is remarkably fat. I have heard

That bugs are very nutritious, contain more protein
Than we give them credit for. For the moment,
We take notes, with good intentions map out
A potentially more involved anthropological inquiry,
Agree amongst ourselves there must be

No contamination. Being eight times their size
Knowledge of us would smother their ambitions.
Our parallel worlds can co-exist as long

As they co-exist in mutual ignorance.
Let us hope there is no gold in these hills,
No manganese to extract. We each will do a book,
Make back our expedition investment with the royalties.
Johnson hollers, look, they all go about
Wondrously, innocently, naked. We could
Include discreet photographs, mix tribal beauties
In with the village snapshots, triple
The sales. After a few years

The public's fascination will wane.
Inevitably, electricity will come to their gully,
And all the tiny people will have to find
Real jobs, give up the insects for shaved beef,
Accept the government dole, wear colorful loincloths;
And, to the varied commissioners
Then coming to ensure that their welfare
Is being maintained - as our world
Supplants theirs even here in nowhere -
Share how they held out for so long.

CASH CROP

When we came to harvest our villagers, we found them to all be cardboard. Expertly cut, and painted so well that, full on, one would not expect them to be other than flesh. Each stood or sat or toiled in an appropriate theme - some outside of cardboard houses, some within. Cardboard children, cardboard pets, cardboard livestock. With closer inspection, they appeared to be shellacked, so that even a moderate rain would not destroy them – though the water beading would show them as representations, not true subjects. Such fine work, and no living villagers to be seen. After our initial amazement and honor of the workmanship, we thought: cardboard villagers - less effort to harvest, lower maintenance, unprecedented docility, even if those gains for us are serendipitous. No one can blame us for not then racing off through the surrounding lands to find villagers to harvest. No one can blame us for locking onto this new, easier cardboard catch. So we took our quota in cardboard: every fifth finely crafted cardboard villager. It was so much easier than corralling live ones: these prey did not complain or barter or fight or run for the hiding places each harvest we already had planned they would likely go. These stacked well, fit more cleanly into the conveyance, had no special requirements in order to survive the journey. For the cycle, we - and possibly the flesh villagers - were happier. Who knows how the market would see it? A day's harvest done in an hour? We will project fantastic-supposed buyer advantages, parade proudly our own new cardboard purchases. What are the many ways a cardboard villager is better than a live villager? How much more service can a new owner imagine? We will be convincing. The market will adapt – it always does. And the villagers, seeing from afar the success of their ruse, will spend the time between harvests building new cardboard villagers, slaving over the shellac and paints and the pliant board. So much work, so much to collect.

COMMON GROUND

This is the savannah
Between two countries where no man
Is allowed to beat his wife.
To the left and the right
Civility reigns. Women
Are protected from those
Who would profess their physical
Mastery in the most openly
Visible and violent ways. We rent

To citizens of our neighbor nations
Space on the savannah by
The square meter, by the half
Hour. Half an hour is always
Enough, though sometimes it takes
More than one square meter. Rates
Are kept reasonable by volume.

We ae not a greedy nation.

We sell tickets to particular plots
At comfort gates stretching drearily
Along the reasonable border fence. We
Are not a populous land, so
We hire women from one neighbor
Nation to man our gates shared with
The nation on the opposite side.

They speak different languages
But have developed a common tongue.

They silently hold out a ticket in
One hand, cup the other for coin.
Usually, the woman entering
Looks back to ask her husband:
One ticket or two.
Exact fare is encouraged.

GIFT

My husband has fashioned me many things of great wonder. A gryphon, our unicorn, the town's signature basilisk. With his ability to re-sequence DNA and a sufficient quantity of raw living cells, there seems no end to what he can accomplish. And no end to his generosity. I have birds with gills, the most pleasant of singing snakes. There are times, though, when I stare idly at my long, glowing fingers and wonder, would he craft more than he can handle?

REGRETS

I took the last whale to a bar on Granby street.
He was not as large as the mythology
Of this very event would have him,
But still the quarters were a bit snug
And a few of the existing patrons
Snarled and offered obscene advice.

No matter.

I was paying cash and ready to go
All the way to empty pockets,
And the barkeep suspected it.
Nothing would be too much for this day.
The whale started out with beer
But soon was doing bourbon and ginger,
Watching me with my low-calorie draft,
Wincing an air of indulgence. I did not know
How much it would take to get a whale drunk,
But I figured for this singular occasion
We would keep pouring until
The blowhole went scratchy

And I could convince him
That French-fries were krill, or he
Would roll over and let bemused
Coeds rub his belly and fondle a flipper.

But drink after drink he kept staring at me:
Me, holding my weak-sister light beer —
And then he would toss back
Another bourbon and ginger

And stare yet some more. Myself,
Six or eight beers into the ritual,
I began to think his stare -
Dry eyed and the same from either side -
Was not a reservoir of indulgence, but
A sterner opinion: perhaps
Forgiveness, perhaps even understanding.
I don't know who drove home,
But that last whale and I have not seen
Each other since, and if anyone at all
Has heard more than the last of him
They are not telling. But they likely know.

LIMITS

The pastor was taken aback when he was asked to perform the ceremony in a bear suit. But then he saw the fairy wings attached to the bride's lizard skin wedding dress, and he shrugged: oh, it was to be that sort of wedding. He imagined the base of it was simply secular, and the religion only for show and a way to get help on the paperwork. The groom would be gaudily costumed as a goat. Pardon, a ram. Appropriate, no doubt. The night after the wedding the couple would be hoping that no one in the hovels around the newly-weds' conjugal night's hammock would get a finger of sleep. Two witnesses, one dressed as Death, one as an iron-clad Aphrodite. Or maybe these were not disguises, costumes, or a wedding dress. The audience would be playing soccer and the wedding itself would take place at the first game stoppage for foul. Vows would be exchanged, admonitions delivered, and the game would be resumed. But what if there were no foul, the pastor asked as he looked up from the over-worn bear costume. Oh, but you don't know the crowd, the curious groom said, and popped the pastor flat in the mouth, though largely in demonstration vice in true violence. Thankfully, the fee was good; and, when at the proposed wedding, the game evidenced no foul – at least none that were called by the distracted officials – he got to keep the fee and negotiate a new fee for the potential nuptials at the game set up for the next available solstice. Same bear suit.

CHANGE OF HEART

The Yeti does not stalk.
It simply walks in,
Finds the sturdiest chair in the room,
And sits.

You eye him in ordered silence,
Your hands distantly occupy each other,
Your thoughts making no sudden moves:
The balance of you chilled into inaction.

No one knows what to do
During fantastic encounters such as this.
You think: not even I knew
That was the sturdiest chair in the room.

CHOOSING

A woman is moving deliberately towards me. She has the long of suns, the thin of oceans. She has the beauty of the indeterminate. Her legs drive aside the grass, bring the air around her near to spinning. Her arms are full, but what she carries seems to be of no weight. I cannot yet see her burden nor her intentions. I imagine her to have the mind of a knife thrower's assistant; the thoughts of a member of the caste that knows the trickery – winks, in her by a thousandth too small costume, at the evergreen safety of peril. I imagine I am the audience; but no, she is moving deliberately, economically towards me. Out of her full arms, with each stride, falls another ghost. Ghost after ghost, evaporating on the unbent grass; untethered, unrecognized. The loss of each ghost a misplayed potential, tatters of inter-dimensional opportunity. I reach laboriously down for the first of my silver-dashed knives.

THE BIRTH OF THE MUNDANE

This is the day that turtles have their revolt.
That circus clowns step out of the shadows and say
"I have alms for you" and wicker forth a fistful of dry leaves.
This is the day of breakfast cereal for dinner.
I have been lonely for now; waiting in the elemental for now;
Stretched as on a lover's rack, flesh burned by the ropes
And every ounce of me screaming for an exhausting
Moment of piety, for now. A galaxy of dust is born just
At the edge of the porch and shouts its free will.
The clowns are distracted and the turtles fight on.
Dogs are putting on lipstick. A cat struts in his best
Sunday suit. Raccoons rise on two legs and high heels.
I sit at the table naked, drawing my future in melon rinds.
The birds on the exposed wires line up in geometries
Fresh from the returned time-traveler, a clockwork of a man
In a sterile uniform, who pats his chest
And says "these are mysteries" then turns to me, lonely until
Now, eying this naked woman at a kitchen table with
Cereal and melon rinds, thinking *a rack*. Please stand back,
I have a decoder ring. Or come forward.
Everyone is prepared and the consequences are stacked
Like props in a mechanical animal circus, covered
Like an under aged victim in geometrically pure free will; and
For the striving, disjointed essence of all of us, success
Is the same furiously inept, pious mathematics in this,
Our moment: now.

SUSTENANCE

I tell the leprechauns to keep a lower profile. The green suits, the shoe bells, must go. The felt hats must go. The talk of rainbows has to be put by. No more stereotypes. No more slaves to the myth. In the beginning, our conversation is civil enough. Close to parlor talk. We swap points of relevance, the mannerisms of meaning; begin to see each other less as caricatures, and more as characters driven by caricature. As my neighbors look in through my large, picture window, I call out to them, advocating with them in their domestic duty, shouting that these leprechauns are not for eating: there is not enough to them to make a proper meal. But then there is a little rain, a return of sun, a rainbow. And, when one leprechaun mentions gold, I think: a knife, a fork, a pot, the smell of boiling appetite hanging in the air like yesterday's laundry. I imagine my neighbors following the little, happy prey unknowingly to riches. Onward: and what would it be for me to snatch one silly, delicious leprechaun loitering at the end of that rainbow bound line?

THE MISUNDERSTANDING

I was telling the mermen
That I did not think
Wife swapping, between us,
Would work. I just
Did not see how it could be
Accomplished, physically:
Either species,
Male; either species,
Female. No amount
Of open-mindedness,
Or raw salt-splintered desire,
Would make up for anatomical
Incompatibility. I was
Telling the mermen that I,
For a non-finned coconspirator,
Was certainly honored
That they thought of us –
A simple couple that had mastered
The mere tip of sea language
At the enclosing glass of their in-town
Vacation home – as sufficiently
Intimate with them for them to be intimate,
Sufficiently, with us: but we were
On uncharted seas.
I am no prude, but science
Was not on the side of our performance.
Then, the nearest merman to the glass
Quite regally lifted my shimmering wife
So her head popped playfully out of the water,

And she drew a body's length of electrical air.
His wife – her skin clutching closely its tatters
Of naked brine and trapped oxygen –
Tapped her language gently on the barrier, as her
Huge, buoyant breasts flashed by unbound,
Why, what did you think we meant?
Come, swim.

THE BROTHERING SPELL

I could build a boat to take all the people away on the water to a new, less worn land. It would have to be a magic boat, one into which all the village could fit. Each person in the village, arriving at the boat, would shrink: first to half his or her size, then to the size of a matchstick. As each arrived, I would watch that person gargle my magic and shrink: then I would pack the person in a box; with soon all the people side to side, and in several boxes. I would load them in the boat mechanically until every family were loaded and I was the last of the village with size. I would push the boat into the currents and then go into my village, carrying in my arms the same magic that made the people small. A hungrily happy magic, a magic that sees nothing but its task. I would use that magic to make the village small and then I would sit: my people adrift as matchsticks, my village a huddlestone of dust, and I would ask myself how else could all my effort have ended, what closing did I expect to my mongering spells?

ADVERTISING PLOY

I do not know
When the crabs had at last had
Enough. Everything had been
Going well: boiling and boiling
And letting my customers watch
As the live crabs are dropped
Hard shelled into the cylindrical pot.
One crab on occasion would
Catch a claw on the rim –
But the steam would soon get him
And into the murdering water he would
Slide. Some customers I suspect
Would root for a crab like that one
To make it out, scurry through
A back door left open for ventilation,
Ride run-off to a storm drain,
Power his way to the sea. No matter.
The customer pays by the half dozen,
Eats him and his crate-mates anyway.
Then, on what should be a busy night,
With crabs and beer giving stench to
The unappreciative businesses to either side
Of our specialty restaurant, we open
The happy door to the room where the live
Crabs are kept and the formidable wooden
Crates are blundered open, wire mesh
Unbent, stretched aside. Under the ledge
Of the storage shelves: dozens of eyes,
The dancing of raised claws, rows
Of decision about how the crabs' night
Ends, why the taste is so legendary.

LISTEN

I hear the voices of the water. Not mermaid voices. Not fish, nor cetacean, voices. A civilization of voices. The soft, careful voices of warriors plotting. The bruised, back of the hand voices of lovers who believe for stern seconds that passion is prized more if it is endless. The battleship-gray voices of mothers disowning their children. The boastful voices of those who have accomplished nothing. The red glowing barn voices of those scheming wealth out of poverty. The gossamer voices of suppression. One voice that believes there are no voices, shouting. A voice hidden in a far-off lagoon, lingering in the shallows like a rifle shot. Brute voices and soft. A community of voices, a society of voices, a civilization of voices, all with mouths at my ear united in one common, tentacled plea: drown, drown.

SOCIALIZATION

Give me a lesson in humility.
Give me a lesson in dignity.
Give me a lesson in the dark sex.
What I learn does not matter.
What matters is the taking to book,
The pencil raised and ready,
Head up, the look of listening.
Give me a lesson in the seven deadly sins.
Tell me what is good, what is bad,
What to avoid, what to embrace.
Tell me.
I smooth the crease of my pants,
Or the folds of my rough skirt.
I think of Jenny the conquered
Or Jeffrey the conqueror.
Give me a lesson on value,
How to assess worth.
Give me a lesson on mortar.
I am only one brick.
Tell me how that which holds us
Together is mixed, then marketed.
I am touching myself
In unmentionable places.
Tell me you need this so to keep
Your bricks from cracking in the sun.
Tell me what a fine house we will become.

HARVEST

Six soldiers sit with their backs to the moon, looking like six chicken legs set out for this Sunday's afternoon family reunion dinner. Six legs from chickens raised on this very farm; chickens that came when rhythmically called; chickens that received feed from the upturned, folded apron of the plaid family matriarch. Chickens that pulled at the ground, where the soldiers blindly sit, for gizzard stones; chickens who wearily chased insects on the land between the soldiers and the moon. And, in the coming morning the rooster will tiredly climb the speckled fence outside of the chicken coop and say, "Oh my sisters, three more have gone." And only now, the soldiers – who are not above simple chicken thievery – notice by moonlight the chicken yard, the yowling hint of a coop. And they believe in feathers.

REGRETS

I work for a dolphin.
Across the hall he folds
Awkwardly into his fake
Leather chair, his head
Far forward of the head rest,
Balanced, leaning on the arm rests,
Rocking restlessly even though
A dolphin in a chair should
Inspire a balance concern, not
Purposeful teetering. Half the time
I cannot understand what his clicks
And shrills mean, and to do my job
I guess at what he needs, what
His idea of progress and deadlines
Might be. It is not so different
From working for anyone.
His boss comes in every so often,
Sometimes carries a pail of fish.
I love the arc of the toss as
He is rewarded. I wish
Everything were so easy.

INTELLIGENCE

The ants we found to be the size of house cats. They wore ruts in the land, created virtual canyons, at times encouraged river beds. The enriching surprise was that the aardvarks were the size of garden spiders. One ant could feed an entire clan of fidgeting aardvarks for weeks. Everywhere there were decaying ant bodies only ten percent consumed, the clan of aardvarks that claimed the kill bravely sated and without means to preserve the meat. The aardvarks morosely move on, a good kill mostly wasted, their plenty burned as sustaining calories; with a need to plan for the next monstrous ant hunt, a need to forget the fellow clan members who in the wondrously coordinated campaign were by one ant – surrendering reluctantly, or gloriously surviving – or another culled from the collective. We have seen the bright in the aardvarks' eyes. We have seen how splendidly they map murder. One day we will make profitable pact with them and plot the demise of these wearying ants, their ruts, the mysticism that is aardvark lore. We will make fabulous sense of this teasing place.

CONCEPTION

I do not bring you sorrow or passion.
I do not bring you joy.
I have no sympathy to give,
No rage. No remembrance,
No ecstasy, no fear, no loathing.
Not even hatred, that bed
Of ashes in the belly
That colors all with the brush
Of inadequacy. Nothing for you
But the lack of regard, the absence
Of disregard, suspension of self,
The hours of timelessness, eons
Of the instantaneous. Love
As an apple in cherished myth.
Take the nothing I give you,
You beautifully gaunt equation,
Make something of it.

ACCOMPLISHMENT

Six yellow dogs consider the long dirt road. There is the porch, the water trough, the food bowl, the dirt road. Grass comes and goes along the dirt road's edges. Too few cars for six dogs. Too few cars for four dogs. Too few cars for two dogs. One dog would not feel slighted by the lack of cars. He could dream what he wanted to dream, rolling in his somnambulant readiness on the careless porch boards. The color of that dream would not matter. He might dream of six dogs, of being the one dog worthy of a car.

THE COVENANT

There is a beautiful woman
Undressing in the Home Depot parking lot.
I am going to watch her.
I have to watch her.
It is a part of my biology.
I have been married many
Many years, and had the wife and I had
Children, this woman could be my daughter.
Her persistent breasts bounce with the effort
Of her casting off her shoes,
Her beginning to unstaple her jeans.
Most people are staring only nervously,
The men with the blood rising in their groins
And the women with thoughts
Of this could be me, or this
Could be my daughter. Do not think long:
We are about to find out
How close she shaves. The end of this
Will be police officers and a blanket.
Imagine a time
When this act would not be illegal,
When any woman could disrobe
In a parking lot inhabited almost
Exclusively by men. Imagine.
But know as well that in the few littoral minutes
Between undress and arrest
This woman will change from a woman
Taking off her clothes to
An entertainment.

She pops out of her jeans
Like the last unspent kernel of corn
In an industrial grade hot air corn popper.
How each of us will notify
Our spouses of this parking lot inconsequence,
Man to man, woman to woman,
Will vary like our descriptions of the last clothing to go.

THE ANGUISH

I know you were with him through all the chambers of the night. His six legs one by one enfolded you, stunning you with surgical precision, while you drummed passion into the sternness of his exoskeleton. His antennae, each as though alive, slipped/probed about your eager shoulders, and your breath rasped across his compound eyes, driving clouds of grieving water vapor along the stuttering surface of his sight. The chattering of his mandibles drew pure iridescence into your engorged heart, and your skin surely grew hot and threaded, and to his every move you were an echo, blind in your release, deaf to all but the hive of your own symphony. In the end, his wings unfolded proudly to give him greater art in balance; and the night was wounded by the quickness of your stinging, meaningless murmurs. All this, the entire bridgeless infidelity, I could forgive had you turned at the moment of measure and with one last mammalian moment, bitten his head off. But no, my love, you did not. And I will not be next.

THE WEDDING PRESENT

I built a house for the dark woods monster.
Three bedroom ranch, energy efficient
Windows, storm doors front and back.
The attached garage can hold
One car and a small work area,
Peg board all around for hand tools
And the lucky, unused yard instruments.
I put in a foundation rather than
A slab, and so there are steps,
Steps to get in, steps to get out,
Steps away from the garage's flimsy interior door.
The neighbors suspect nothing.
All work is to code,
And I pay the neighbors' children
To keep the grass in check, fix
The flower beds when weeds break out.
Now and again someone might see
Something strange at a window,
Catch the door knob rattling, wonder
Why no one answers the bell.
A few are positively put off
By the failure to cherish their knocks.
No one thinks the place is vacant,
And at night there are lights,
And me once a week struggling to bring in groceries.
I did not do it out of my goodness,
Nor out of concern for the deep woods monster,
Nor to save all the silly potential victims
Domesticating him would leave

Free to roam the deep woods to no bad end.
No. I did it for you.
I did it for our plans,
The projected return on investment.
I can imagine myself years from now,
Ready for the last dry stages of matrimony,
A man of means and character,
Locked in the traditions of my circumstance:
The formal man one day with his formal
Betrothed having always this place
And its evil, stunted resident
To fall back on, a place to carry my love
Through the low rent door and into
The favor of my long-supported monster,
Both of us elated that we have come to this accommodation at last.
And the three of us then will feast
Each on the other until there are only two,
And one might not be me, and one might not be you.

STUDY IN LUCK

An old drive-in, with the sound box unclipped from a pole and hung inside the car window by the same clip. Bodies sitting close as on the huge screen massive images move like elephants in love. Bodies sitting close is the important element: the car a mobile motel room with the excuse of a movie. Might as well rent a room and pretend you are there just to watch the television together. There you could get more naked. But no one at the drive-in cares how naked you get. The movie runs on, every couple is preoccupied with each other's hands. Then, just like last week, the intergalactic portal opens in your back seat and the Zorgarin researcher suspends himself two inches above the faux leather bench seat, staring at the two of you entangled in the front. You ignore him, as your hand is about to go slithering skin to skin. He has seen this movie before, but nonetheless he pulls out his service recorder and starts taking field notes.

THE MATE

I am not the woman you are looking for.

Here, let me introduce the botanist.
He has identified hundreds
Of previously unknown species.
His wife is a flower that blooms
Only along a six mile stretch
Of the upper Amazon. He goes there
But once a year, for sex; and yet
They remain a couple.

All the rest of the year
The botanist's wife is a green
Hollow reed at river side.
Not all of the details are known
But the botanist is sure
His wife blooms only once per year
And only when he is there
To commit the conjugal act:
To bring man to plant, plant to man.

I am not the woman you are looking for.

The botanist writes of their relationship.
His scientific papers are politely published
In all the world's top journals.
He lectures.
Boys attend the lectures and sit in the back
Imagining the crisp flowering of the botanist's wife.
The botanist is unaware of this.
He believes the boys, yes, even the entire audience,

Revel in the sense of wonder, the discovery
Of the whole-cloth rare. The boys shift
Nervously. A woman at the front
Asks how the bloom withstands his passion,
How the species sustains itself
In the loneliness of its independent genes.

That is the woman you are looking for.
She is here for a day, and then gone.
Let me take you to her. It is
An arduous trip, a trip through endless
Hollow reeds, and along treacherous
Light in the shallows of river banks.

And once you find her,
You find that she blooms but once a year.

MELDING

A paying robot is still a customer. She shuts off her darkly red advertising lamp, steps back from the doorway, lets him mechanically shuffle past her into the blue-hued room. By reflex, she double checks the cash in hand, places it in the near bureau drawer. With as calm and metrical voice as she can manage, she asks to see the programming for the subroutine she will be servicing. It will tell her if they need the bed, or a chair, or if this encounter will simply occur in standing room only.

DEVELOPING PAPER DOLLS

We are fine figurines,
Paper cut in one unending motion,
Our intricacies no more
Than proof of talent.
The imaginary in an imagined world:
A concatenation of two-dimensional carpenters, businesswomen,
Plumbers, mothers, accountants,
Fairies and pole dancers,
All held together by being
Pulled of one continuous sheet.

Paper cut in so much detail cannot last.
I can feel in my cellulose
What rending will do to us,
What we will be as mere material.

And then more paper,
Folded over and over,
Folded into armies,
The independence of physical limitations,
The interdependence of craft
And method, tools and tinkering,
Folded back in against itself:
Equal, harmonious, even when poorly cut.

Discover this art.
Invite us into your world.
Give us names,
Seduce us into your first kiss,
Think of our sex as something you have made yourself,

Then think you can do it again,
At will again and again,
The scissors agape with wonder.

ACCESSORY

I hire a boy to help with the large shadows. He works cheap, and I dare not ask my accountant how we escape minimum wage laws. It is good training for him, practically a Victorian style apprenticeship. I start him out with jobs he can never accomplish. He must learn failure, the feeling of being saddled with four left feet, or trapped by giants. Only then can he appreciate the mundane right-sizing of success. He folds the far corners of ordinary working-class house shadows as they stretch across humiliating backyards. I start at the base, where the shadow connects to the house. Slowly. Slowly. I do not want to overtake him. Though I retire my speed, the two of us together still accomplish more in less time. He focuses like a mirror no child of his age should be able to stash expendable dark into. In a few weeks, I will let him harvest an uncomplicated shadow all by himself. An electrical transformer. Perhaps a meticulously trimmed hedge. I shout for him to roll tighter where the chimney dusk extends about the roof's gracefully longing, solid ebony. Yes, one day far from now he will likely be able to snatch the shadows of birds. To my direction he smiles, then opens his mouth to reveal the prevailing dark within. One day, he will gather even that internal dark to place on his poverties and pleasures shelf, arranging the lathered wind of it so that it stands in opposition to the space it gargles. But, for now, he is inexpensive help – though ceding him the experience that my work with him provides, perhaps I am paying too much. I point with my shadowless hand to where next he should spend his grasp, and he stretches forward quite like unquestioningly I once did in my brilliant, light-loving innocence. For now, he will do.

CUSTOMS

It is nine o'clock
And you know soon there will be
The usual knock, the simple
Pleasantries, the idle small talk
That leads from nothing to nowhere.
You will let the wolf in. Here,
You will say, have a sniff
At the pretzels, let me turn off
The television. Oh no, just a rerun
Of a variety show. Please
Pull that old pillow out
From the green chair, curl up,
Make yourself comfortable.
And the wolf, as he has
A thousand previous nights,
Will do all this. At every
Rehearsed move you will search
For a sign in his breathing,
Look for a new lack of economy
In his motions. The wolf
Will sigh, tell you this is not a land
For wolves anymore, that your kind
Has stitched certainty dawn to dawn,
The suddenness of unsettled conflict
Has crept beaten into settled history.
There is no longer a place for his kind.

You will pretend to hear nothing
As the pack unlatches the door

To the chicken coop, one more night
As every night, noses amongst your chickens
For the best. Just one to share,
So the cost is not too great to bear.

The wolf notes it is getting late,
Has finished only half his beer,
Taken none of the pretzels,
Unwinds himself from the chair
And offers a paw, a slight nod.

Waiting next door for the wolf's visitation,
Your neighbor is rocking on his porch,
Lemonade and two glasses on a table beside.
All about town, in every instance, there is a difference.

OTHER BOOKS BY KEN POYNER:

Constant Animals, flash fiction

The Book of Robot, speculative poetry

Victims of a Failed Civics, speculative poetry

Avenging Cartography, flash fiction

The Revenge of the House Hurlers, flash fiction

Engaging Cattle, flash fiction

Stone the Monsters, or Dance, speculative poetry

Lessons from Lingering Houses, speculative poetry

Both *The Book of Robot* and *Stone the Monsters, or Dance* were Elgin award nominees in their original publication year.

www.ingramcontent.com/pod-product-compliance
Lightning Source LLC
LaVergne TN
LVHW051749080426
835511LV00018B/3277